WHO IS CUTER?

Baby Anteater or Baby Tapir?

by Mari Schuh

BLASTOFF! READERS 1

BLASTOFF! READERS, AN IMPRINT OF BELLWETHER MEDIA BY FLUTTERBEE

Blastoff! Readers are carefully developed by literacy experts to build reading stamina and move students toward fluency by combining standards-based content with developmentally appropriate text.

LEVELS

Level 1 provides the most support through repetition of high-frequency words, light text, predictable sentence patterns, and strong visual support.

Level 2 offers early readers a bit more challenge through varied sentences, increased text load, and text-supportive special features.

Level 3 advances early-fluent readers toward fluency through increased text load, less reliance on photos, advancing concepts, longer sentences, and more complex special features.

★ **Blastoff! Universe**

Reading Level

Blastoff! Beginners — Grade K

Blastoff! Readers — Grades 1–3

Blastoff! Discovery — Grade 4

This edition first published in 2027 by Bellwether Media, Inc.

For information regarding permission, write to Bellwether Media, Inc., Attention: Permissions Department, 3500 American Blvd W, Suite 150, Bloomington, MN 55431.

Library of Congress Cataloging-in-Publication Data is available at www.loc.gov or upon request from the publisher.

ISBN: 9798898800215 (hardcover)
ISBN: 9798898801458 (ebook)

Editor: Rachael Barnes Designer: Jennifer Bowyer

Printed in the United States of America, North Mankato, MN.

Table of Contents

Pups and Calves!	4
Stripes and Spots	8
Growing Up	14
Who Is Cuter?	20
Glossary	22
To Learn More	23
Index	24

Pups and Calves!

Baby anteaters are called pups. Baby tapirs are called calves.

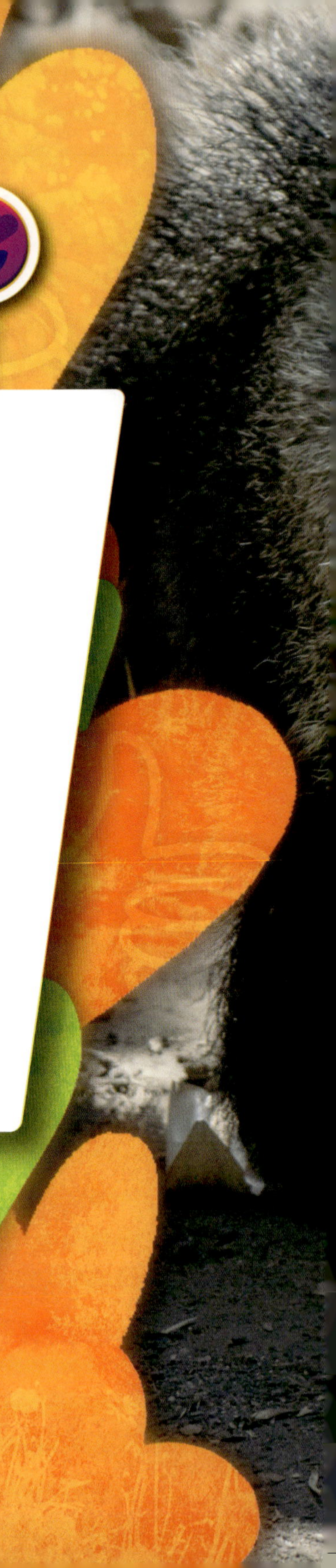

pup
calf

Both babies are
born with hair.
Both babies have
snouts that stand out!

snout

Stripes and Spots

Calves are born
with stripes and spots.
Pups have stripes.
They match mom!

stripes and spots
stripes

Calves have
short tails.
Pup tails
are longer.

tail

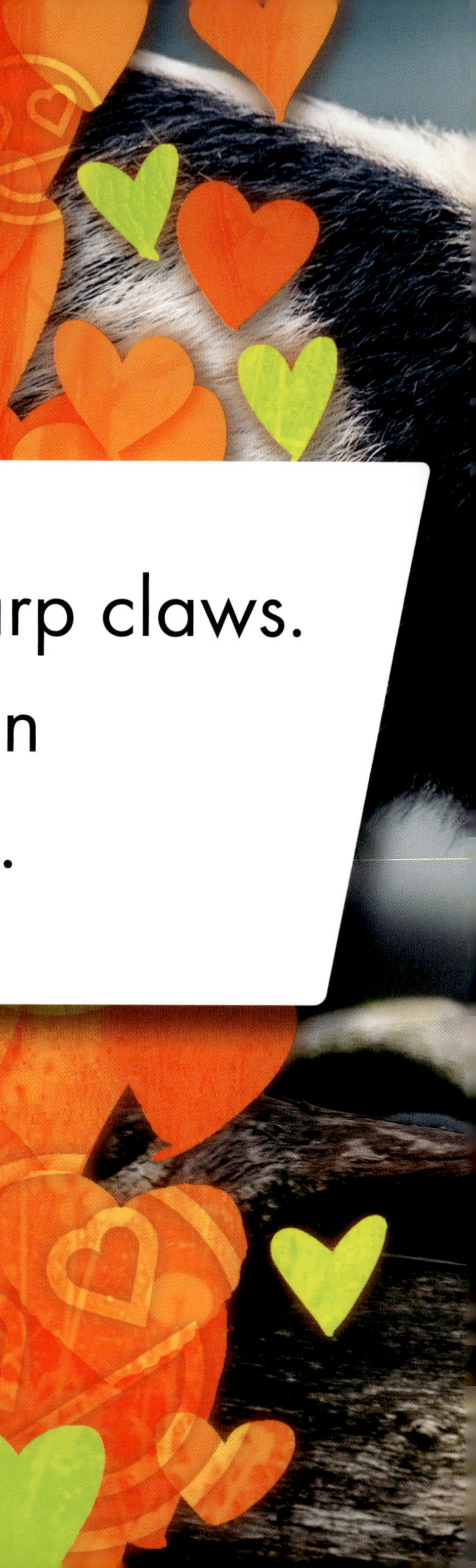

Pups have sharp claws. Calves walk on hard **hooves**.

hooves
claw

Growing Up

Calves pick up food with their bendy snouts. Pups catch ants with their long, sticky tongues!

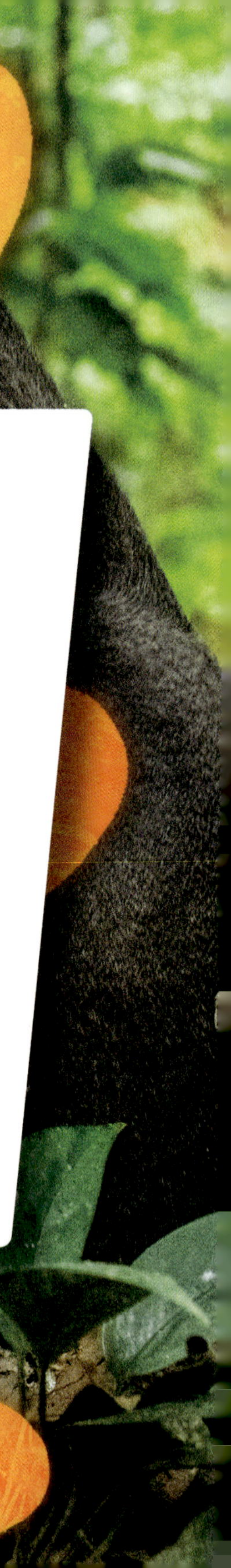

tongue

Calves lose their stripes and spots. They **fade**. Pups keep their stripes.

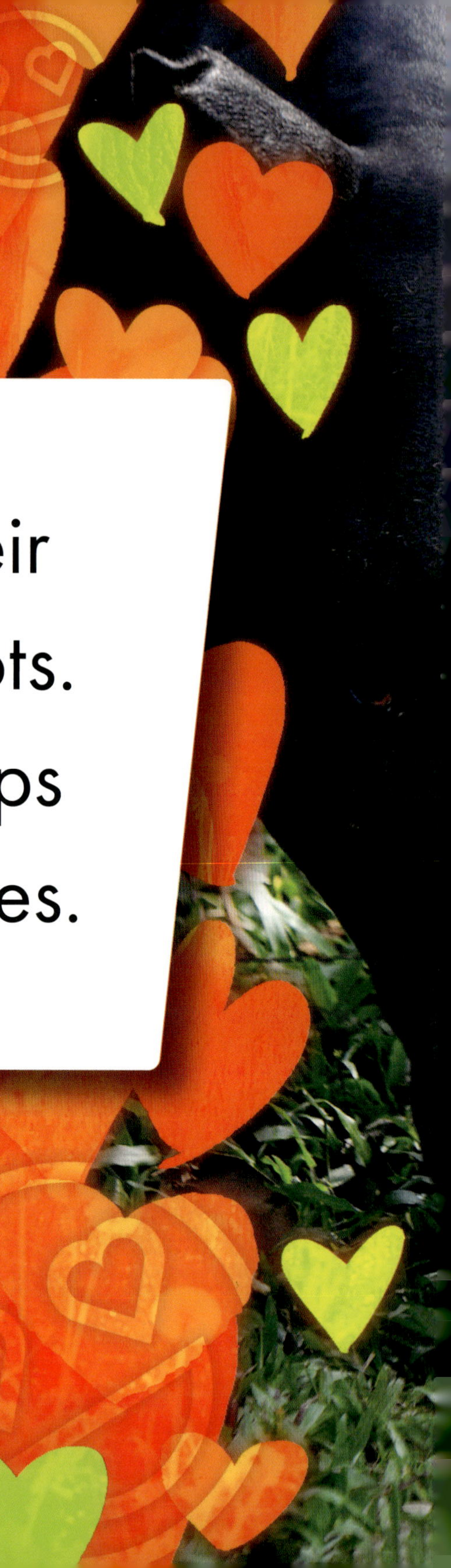

fading spots

Pups climb
on mom's back.
Calves stand
soon after birth.
Who is cuter?

Who Is Cuter?

Baby Anteater

Who is your pick?
Vote at
BellwetherMedia.com

Baby Tapir

Glossary

fade

to slowly go away

hooves

hard coverings on the feet of some animals

snouts

the noses and mouths of some animals

To Learn More

AT THE LIBRARY

Grack, Rachel. *Giant Anteaters*. Minneapolis, Minn.: Bellwether Media, 2024.

Grack, Rachel. *Tapirs*. Minneapolis, Minn.: Bellwether Media, 2024.

Schuh, Mari. *Aardvark or Anteater?* Minneapolis, Minn.: Bellwether Media, 2023.

ON THE WEB

FACTSURFER

Factsurfer.com gives you a safe, fun way to find more information.

1. Go to www.factsurfer.com.
2. Enter "baby anteater or baby tapir" into the search box and click 🔍.
3. Select your book cover to see a list of related content.

Index

anteaters, 4
claws, 12, 13
food, 14
hair, 6
hooves, 12, 13
mom, 8, 18
snouts, 6, 7, 14
spots, 8, 9, 16, 17
stripes, 8, 9, 16
tails, 10, 11
tapirs, 4
tongues, 14, 15

The images in this book are reproduced through the courtesy of: Ian Bottle, front cover (anteater); Signature Message, front cover (tapir); Eric Isselee, pp. 3 (anteater, tapir), 20 (main anteater), 21 (main tapir); Azahara Perez/ Alamy, pp. 4-5; Mark Malkinson/ Alamy, pp. 5, 6-7; ZSSD/ Minden Pictures, pp. 7, 20 (catches ants); imageBROKER/Torsten Antoniewski/ Alamy, pp. 8-9; Junko Kimura/ Staff/ Getty Images, p. 9; Honza123, pp. 10-11; Nick Garbutt/ Nature Picture Library, p. 11; Kacper Rzepecki/ Getty Images, pp. 12-13; tatianaput, p. 13; Nature Picture Library/ Nick Hawkins/ Alamy, pp. 14-15; Nature Picture Library/ Edwin Giesbers/ Alamy, p. 15; IMAGO/IMAGO/Then Chih Wey/ Alamy, pp. 16-17; mauritius images GmbH/ Gerard Lacz/ Alamy, p. 17; Sean Crane/ Minden Pictures, pp. 18-19; J.NATAYO, pp. 19, 21 (stands soon after birth); Nick Garbutt/ Minden Pictures, p. 20 (climbs on mom); mirecca, p. 20 (keeps stripes); Xinhua/ Alamy, pp. 21 (loses stripes and spots), 22 (fade); dangdumrong, p. 21 (grabs food with snout); Azoor Wildlife Photo/ Alamy, p. 22 (hooves); Diego Grandi, p. 22 (snouts).